Myth and Miracle

An Essay on the
Mystic Symbolism
of Shakespeare

by

G. Wilson Knight

LONDON
ED. J. BURROW & CO., LTD.
43, 45 & 47 Kingsway

Printed in England
by
Ed. J. Burrow & Co. Ltd.,
Cheltenham.

PREFACE.

The thesis of this essay was first published as a short article, entitled " The Poet and Immortality," in *The Shakespeare Review* for October, 1928. Before that I had developed it at some length as an essay, with the addition of discursive notes, under the title *Thaisa*, which failed to reach publication. It is, I believe, still searching for recognition in America. Here I indicate only the bare outlines of my view, and the necessity of my contention may not be clearly apparent until I have published many papers on the various plays and themes of the Shakespeare progress. I express my gratitude for their kindness to those Editors who have already helped me by publishing, accepting, or encouraging my work.

The debt of the present essay to the orthodoxies of Shakespeare criticism, past and current, is, I think, slight. My purpose of poetic interpretation derives from a long-standing dissatisfaction with the usual commentaries. But, though I must alone remain responsible for my reading of the Final Plays, I would like to take this opportunity of acknowledging an influence elsewhere from the work of Mr. J. Middleton Murry.

G. W. K.

Cheltenham, May, 1929.

The superior figures refer
to " Notes " on p. 32

I.

In this essay I shall consider the Final Plays, whose significance has not yet been recognised, as the culmination of a series which starts about the middle of Shakespeare's writing career and exposes to a careful analysis a remarkable coherence and significance; and, by throwing them into direct relation with their predecessors, show that those improbabilities of plot texture and curiosities of the supernatural descending on the purely human interest—as in *Pericles* and *Cymbeline*—are not the freaks of a wearied imagination, as has been usually supposed; nor the work of that convenient " incompetent coadjutor " who is too often at hand when necessary to solve the difficulties of Shakespeare interpretation; but rather the inevitable development of the questioning, the pain, the profundity and grandeur of the plays they succeed. My method is to regard the plays as they stand in the order to which modern scholarship has assigned them;[1] to refuse to regard " sources " as exerting any limit to the significance of the completed work of art; to avoid the side-issues of Elizabethan and Jacobean manners, politics, patronage, audiences, revolutions and explorations; to fix attention solely on the poetic quality and human interest of the plays concerned. Secondary considerations necessarily condition the materials of a poet's work: but it is in the nature of his accomplishment within and transcending those limits that we must always search for the lasting significance of either poet or prophet. For this reason, though I refer to the author of the plays as Shakespeare, I leave any discussion of the questions of consciousness and unconsciousness, intention and inspiration, as unnecessary to a purely philosophic analysis of

the text. To the critic of the poetry the word " Shakespeare " stands alone for the dynamic life that persists
in the plays, and any other " Shakespeare " is a pure
abstraction. We should avoid irrelevancies. That
spiritual quality which alone causes great work to endure
through the centuries should be the primary object of
our attention ; and that quality is implicit in the printed
page. My method is empirically justified : where other
commentators have found incoherence and the inevitable
" incompetent coadjutor," it will show, wherever the
Shakespearean rhythm or metaphor rings true, order,
reason, and necessity.

II.

It has often been observed that *Hamlet*[2] reflects a
mind in pain and perplexity ; so, in different ways, do
Troilus and Cressida and *Measure for Measure*. In *Hamlet*
we are confronted by that mode of the spirit which sees
the world of men and nature as an " unweeded garden " ;
bereft of vision, tortured by too much thinking, obsessed
with love's impurity and death's hideousness. In *Troilus
and Cressida* the same idea recurs with reference to the
frailty of romantic love. Both in the matter of love and
death the thinking in these plays is essentially a time-
thinking. Immortality of the spirit in time and decay
of the body in time are both fearful to Hamlet ; the
inability of love to stand the test of time is a torture to
Hamlet and Troilus. It is as though in these two plays
all higher values were enslaved, and " injurious Time "
enthroned supreme, their antagonist and victor. In
Measure for Measure the pain is less ; the light of a pure
Christian ethic[3] shines through the play, and there is
forecast of the stoic philosophy of the tragedies to follow.

6

But the sex-satire is again powerful. Lucio, the foul-minded and careless wit, continues the Hate-theme which makes Hamlet cry out against the universe as unclean, and which in the figure of Thersites receives one of its clearest and most exaggerated manifestations :

> " Lechery, lechery ! Still, wars and lechery ; nothing else holds fashion : a burning devil take them ! " (V, ii, 195.)

This Hate-theme, closely connected with time-thinking, and inimical to romance and religion and value, as such, eats into the thought of these plays, blighting, decaying. It is evident in the pain of Hamlet, the railings of Thersites, and the disgusting wit of Lucio. It cannot smell the rose for knowledge of the dung in which it was nurtured. *Othello*, which followed these plays, demands a different kind of analysis from its predecessors and successors in Shakespeare's progress in view of its extreme classicism, its concentration on form, its purely æsthetic impact.[4] But it may be observed in passing that its plot perfectly crystalises the thought of the preceding plays : the devil of cynicism, Iago—in whom is combined much of Hamlet, Thersites, and Lucio—causes the hero to distrust the thing of purity and innocence. Desdemona is betrayed, and Othello has slain the thing he loved.

Othello thus completes the first group, the group of problem plays : plays which reflect what William James calls " the sick soul." But if *Othello* completes this group, it as surely heralds the next. The next group, by viewing life in terms of passion and tragedy, gives a solution, as satisfactory as the solution of tragedy may be, to the baffled questions which preceded. It is a mistake to regard such plays as *Macbeth* and *Lear* as in essence pessimistic. Where humanity is shown as intrinsically grand, and his stage is the battleground of a mighty conflict, there is purpose and a noble destiny : where these things are in evidence there is no room for "the sick soul," and, conversely, "the sick soul" has no knowledge of these things. *Macbeth* and *Lear* are characterised by the thunder of tragedy, and the mystery of eternity broods over a tragic close. The pessimistic and painful impact of *Troilus and Cressida* is largely due to the fact that the hero and heroine are left remorselessly alive : death would lend pathos and open vistas of eternity where pathos and eternity were not wanted. High tragedy and cynicism are incompatible. In *Macbeth* and *Lear* the Shakespearean symbol of tragic conflict—the storm or tempest—which had lent splendour to *Julius Caesar*, but had been avoided in the problem plays and only curiously and half-heartedly wedged into the plot of *Othello*, now recurs in full force. Storm in the elements accompanies the thunder and lightning of the passionate heart of man. In *Lear* the suffering of mankind is sublimated into a noble, stoic destiny : Lear, Gloucester, Cordelia, Kent, Edgar, the Fool, endure their lot, and are aureoled with the halo of suffering. The play is a play of "creative suffering." All, it is to be noted, are brought by their own pain to a noble and exquisite apprehension of the pain of others : Hamlet thought only of himself. *Lear*, too, goes far to answer the questions of *Hamlet* on the matter of death. In *Lear* death is the end. There is no time-thinking of immortality. "Break heart, I prithee break," says Kent over Lear. Death is the sweet ender of suffering, and we are at peace with it, as we were never at peace with it in *Hamlet*. In the same way the Hate-theme of the earlier plays is given sublimity and tremendous meaning in *Timon*. Timon is the grand and universal hater—but only because he is by nature the grand and universal lover. The Hate-theme is thus seen to be born of the aspiring spirit of man, un-at-home in its frail sepulchre of flesh, reaching out to infinity, crying for death because the world is unworthy :

> My long sickness
> Of health and living now begins to mend,
> And nothing brings me all things.

(V, i, 189.)

In *Timon of Athens*—a great and neglected play—we are at peace with the sordidness and foulness of mankind. Again, the tempestuous passion of the hero is its own justification, and the close gives to the action the tragic framework of eternity. All these plays are to the reader, what they must have been to the author, revelations of profundity and grandeur : the mystery of human fate—though still a mystery to the intellect—is intuitively apprehended as we endure to the end of great tragedy. In essence, our understanding is a mystic understanding, and our sense of victory a mystic joy. Tragedy and our religion are inter-significant. The Christian Cross is only the symbol of the Greatest of Tragedies.

Now it is important that we should observe the tremendous advance in optimism and the mystic apprehension of the tragic sacrifice which is marked by the next tragedy, *Antony and Cleopatra*. Death is here sublimated as the supreme good, and directly related to the theme of love. The protagonists, *Antony and Cleopatra*, it has been well said, " die into love."[5] The love-problems and death-problems are resolved by being harmonised in the unity of death-in-love. It is difficult to speak adequately of the last two acts of this perhaps the greatest but one of Shakespeare's plays. In the cold forms of conceptual thought one can say that by synchronising a fine moment of love-consciousness with the time-vanquishing act of death the timeless nature of that love-consciousness is made apparent ; or that the death and love union represents a vision of immortality in terms of quality rather than quantity, of value rather

than time. But the language of conceptual thought fails
before the transcendent reality of this death-revelation.
It must suffice to emphasize the mystic nature of that
vision, and its tragic purification of the diseased love-satire
of the problem plays. And one more fact must be noticed.
The tempest and storm symbolism of the earlier great
tragedies does not recur in *Antony and Cleopatra*, but
gives place to a new mystic symbolism in the music that
preludes the final sacrifice of love :

4 Soldier :	Peace ! what noise ?
1 Soldier :	List, list !
2 Soldier :	Hark !
1 Soldier :	Music i' the air.
3 Soldier :	Under the earth.
4 Soldier :	It signs well, does it not ?
3 Soldier :	No.
1 Soldier :	Peace, I say !
	What should this mean ?
2 Soldier :	'Tis the god Hercules, whom Antony loved,
	Now leaves him.

(IV, iii, 12.)

The emergence of this music-symbolism[6] at this moment
of the tragedy is all-important for our understanding of
the third group of plays. The furthest limit of direct
representation is here reached : tragedy is merging into
mysticism, and what is left to say must be said in terms
not of tragedy, but of miracle and myth. The inner truth
of the tragic fact will thus be explicated in the narratives
of the last plays from *Pericles* to *The Tempest*, and their
plots will reflect the poet's intuition of immortality and
conquest within apparent death and failure : I will now
notice the themes of miracle and music in those plays.

III

The stories of *Pericles* and *The Winter's Tale* are remarkably alike. In both the hero loses his wife and daughter just after the birth of his child ; in both the idea of a child's helplessness is synchronised with a sea-storm of the usual Shakespearean kind ; in both the wife and child are miraculously restored after a long passage of time ; and the revival of Thaisa, and the restoration of Marina and Hermione are accompanied by music. These plays are throughout impregnated by an atmosphere of mysticism. The theology is pseudo-Hellenistic. The Delphic oracle and a prophetic dream occur in *The Winter's Tale ;* Hermione is restored to Leontes in a " chapel " to the sound of music, Thaisa to Pericles in the temple of Diana, with the full circumstance of religious ceremonial. The goddess Diana appears to Pericles. A reader sensitive to poetic atmosphere must necessarily feel the awakening light of some religious or metaphysical truth symbolised in the plot and attendant machinery of these two plays.

Cerimon, who raises Thaisa from the dead, is a recluse and visionary :

> I hold it ever,
> Virtue and cunning were endowments greater
> Than nobleness and riches : careless heirs
> May the two latter darken and expend ;
> But immortality attends the former,
> Making a man a god.

(III, ii, 26.)

The body of Thaisa, supposed dead, is cast ashore by the tempest in a coffin. Cerimon, by his magic, and with the aid of fire and music, revives her :

Well said, well said ; the fire and cloths.
The rough and woeful music that we have,
Cause it to sound, beseech you.
The viol once more : how thou stirr'st, thou
    block !
The music there !—I pray you, give her air.
Gentlemen,
This queen will live : nature awakes ; a warmth
Breathes out of her : she hath not been entranced
Above five hours : see how she 'gins to blow
Into life's flower again !   (III, ii, 87.)

This incident, with the exquisite conception of the character of Cerimon, and the reviving of Thaisa, is one of the pinnacles of Shakespeare's art : this scene and those of the restoration to Pericles of his long-lost daughter and consort which follow, are alone sufficient to establish my thesis that the author is moved by vision, not fancy; is creating not merely entertainment, but myth in the Platonic sense. Now the theme of music again occurs in the meeting of Pericles with Marina :

Pericles :   Now, blessing on thee ! rise ; thou
    art my child.
    Give me fresh garments. Mine own,
    Helicanus ;
    She is not dead at Tarsus, as she
    should have been,
    By savage Cleon: she shall tell thee all;
    When thou shalt kneel, and justify
    in knowledge
    She is thy very princess. Who is
    this ?

Helicanus :   Sir, 'tis the governor of Mytilene,
    Who, hearing of your melancholy
    state,
    Did come to see you.

Pericles :	I embrace you.
	Give me my robes. I am wild in my beholding.
	O heavens, bless my girl ! But, hark, what music ?
	Tell Helicanus, my Marina, tell him
	O'er, point by point, for yet he seems to doubt,
	How sure you are my daughter. But, what music ?
Helicanus :	My lord, I hear none.
Pericles :	None !
	The music of the spheres ! List, my Marina.
Lysimachus :	It is not good to cross him ; give him way.
Pericles :	Rarest sounds ! Do ye not hear ?
Lysimachus :	My lord, I hear. (Music.)
Pericles :	Most heavenly music !
	It nips me unto listening, and thick slumber
	Hangs upon mine eyes : let me rest. (Sleeps.) (V, i, 215.)

The blindness of past Shakespearean criticism is at no point more completely in evidence than in the comments on this play. To the discerning mind it will be evident that we are here confronted with the furthest reach of Shakespeare's poetic and visionary power : if we except the *Tempest*, the latter half of *Pericles* has no equivalent in transcendental apprehension in all Shakespeare but the latter half of *Antony and Cleopatra* which on the plane of myth and symbolism it may be considered to interpret.

Almost of an equal beauty is the restoration of Thaisa in the Temple of Diana.

Cerimon :	. . . . . Look, Thaisa is Recovered.

13

Thaisa :	O, let me look !
	If he be none of mine, my sanctity
	Will to my sense bend no licentious ear,
	But curb it, spite of seeing. O, my lord,
	Are you not Pericles ? Like him you spake,
	Like him you are : did you not name a tempest,
	A birth and death ?
Pericles :	The voice of dead Thaisa !
Thaisa :	That Thaisa am I, supposed dead
	And drown'd.
Pericles :	Immortal Dian !
Thaisa :	Now I know you better.
	When we with tears parted Pentapolis,
	The King, my father, gave you such a ring. (Shows a ring.)
Pericles :	This, this : no more, you gods ! your present kindness
	Makes my past miseries sports. . . .
	(V, iii, 26.)

That last thought of Pericles is to be echoed again, with clear religious and universal significance, in *The Vision of Jupiter* in *Cymbeline*. Now if, as is probable, the greater part of *Pericles* is the work of Shakespeare grafted on to an earlier play of different authorship, of which signs are apparent in some of the early scenes,[7] it is not surprising that, after his composition of these supreme latter acts, he found another plot of the same kind for his next play ; nor is it surprising that that next play, *The Winter's Tale*, though more perfect as a whole, lacks something of the paradisal radiance of *Pericles*. The great artist does not well to repeat himself : in *Pericles*, as the writer handles an old theme, some mystic apprehension of a life that conquers death has sprung to vivid form, as it were, spontaneously : a shaft of light penetrating into the very heart of Death. The studied repetition that follows is less vital. It will be sufficient here to point the recurrence of the themes of birth, restoration, tempest, and music, and to speak shortly of their significance in both plays.

In *The Winter's Tale* the plot turns on Leontes' distrust of Hermione's conjugal loyalty. Now too much stress cannot be laid on the importance attached to infidelity in Shakespeare. The horror at the passing of love's faith is twin to the horror of death : the difficulty is quite as much a metaphysical as a moral one—Troilus cannot understand the patent fact of its existence. In *Hamlet* and *Troilus* these death and love problems are given dramatic form, and leave us distressed ; in *Othello* the faithlessness theme is crystalized into a perfected classic mould and makes a great play, but, since Desdemona dies untrusted, leaves us still pained. In *Antony and Cleopatra*, though the love of the protagonists is shown to us as untrusting, and untrustworthy, a spiritual and passionate thing tossed tempestuously on the waters of temporal existence, yet, by the synchronising of faith with death, we are left with a vision of a timeless instantaneous ascension in death to love, which is life. This tragic apprehension is explicated in narrative form in the parables of *Pericles* and *The Winter's Tale*. Leontes is guilty of Othello's distrust, and thinks Hermione dead. He suffers years of remorse, but at last she is restored to him, in a temple, with ceremony, and to the sounds of music. In Shakespeare the failing of love's faith is essentially a metaphysical difficulty, and one with the difficulty of loss in death : conversely, " perfect love casteth out fear." The infidelity theme of *The Winter's Tale* is thus not essentially different from the loss of Thaisa at sea. In both we see the tempests of temporal conditions seemingly at war with the otherness of a purely spiritual experience.

In both these plays we have the theme of a child bereft of its mother and threatened by storm and thunder. The emphasis on tempests is insistent, and the suggestion is clearly that of the pitifulness and helplessness of humanity born into a world of tragic conflict. That the tempest is percurrent in Shakespeare as a symbol of tragedy need not be demonstrated here at length. Its symbolic significance is patent from the earliest to the latest of the plays—in metaphor, in simile, in long or short descriptions, in stage directions. The individual soul is the " bark " putting out to sea in a " tempest " : the image occurs again and again. For instance, we have in *Macbeth*,

> Though his bark cannot be lost,
> Yet it shall be tempest-toss'd (I, iii, 24),

and in *Timon of Athens* (V, i, 204), we hear of

> . . . other incident throes
> That nature's fragile vessel doth sustain
> In life's uncertain voyage. . . .

and in *Pericles*, which contains perhaps the finest of Shakespeare's profuse storm-poetry in III, i, Marina says (IV, i, 18) :

> Ay me ! poor maid,
> Born in a tempest, when my mother died,
> This world to me is like a lasting storm,
> Whirring me from my friends.

Numerous other references could be given. The theme of helpless childhood synchronised with storm in *Pericles* and *The Winter's Tale* (III, i ; III, iii) is significant, just as the tempests in *Julius Caesar*, *Macbeth* and *Lear* are significant : poetic symbols of the storm and stress of human life, the turbulence of temporal events reflecting and causing tempestuous passion in the heart of man. Lastly, in these two plays we have the music which accompanies resurrection and re-union. This music may seem to perform a dual function : first, to suggest, as a symbol of pure æsthetic delight, the mystic nature of the act being performed ; second, to anæsthetise the critical faculty, as does the overture in a theatre, and prepare the mind for some extraordinary event. But these are in reality twin aspects of the same function : for music, like erotic sight, raises the consciousness until it is in tune with a reality beyond the reach of wisdom. " Music, moody food of us that trade in love," says Cleopatra. Music in Shakespeare is ever the solace and companion of love, and love in Shakespeare the language of mysticism. For this reason the mystic happenings in these plays are accompanied by the theme of music. I will now pass to the third of the mythical plays, *Cymbeline*.

Many of the former elements recur in *Cymbeline*. We have the faithlessness theme in which Posthumus distrusts Imogen, and Iago is resuscitated in the deceiver Iachimo. Posthumus' very name suggests the birth theme of the two former plays : like Marina and Perdita he is cast unprotected into a hostile world. Cymbeline's long-lost sons, Guiderius and Arviragus, remind us of the lost children of Pericles and Leontes. We have again the idea of the apparently dead found to be alive. Guiderius and Arviragus think Imogen is dead, and even prepare to bury her. Solemn music sounds at her supposed death. Posthumus, too, is led to think Imogen dead independently. The same themes are evidently running in the poet's mind, but it is as though the artist tries hard to control them, to control the more directly religious apprehension that is beginning to make the writing of a normal play an impossibility. And this repressed instinct—if repressed it was—certainly has its revenge. In *The Vision of Jupiter* we have Shakespeare's clearest statement in terms of anthropomorphic theology of the significance of the themes I have been analysing in the final plays. Without analysis of the sequence of tragedies and myths the scene will appear dramatically unnecessary and crude : with knowledge of Shakespeare's state of mind in the writing of this play, when his imagination must have been burningly conscious not alone of human life, but of the mystic significance of it, which he had already touched in *Antony and Cleopatra* and *Pericles*, we shall find it quite reasonable that he should attempt a universal statement in direct language concerning the implications of his plot. The scene becomes, in fact, a priceless possession to the interpreter of Shakespeare. It has been often allotted in the past to the " incompetent coadjutor." I will shortly notice this, the central and, for the purpose of this paper, by far the most important, scene in the play.

Posthumus, in the depth of his misery and remorse, sleeps in prison. He has prayed to heaven to take his life, and finally called on his love, whom he has mistrusted, whom he believes dead through his fault :

O Imogen !
I'll speak to thee in silence.   (V, iv, 29.)

There is next a lengthy stage direction, with a three times iterated mention of music. Posthumus' father, mother, and two brothers appear. And these figures chant, to a haunting dirge-like tune of words, a piteous complaint to Jupiter. It is important to observe the universal significance of their words, and its direct bearing on the troubles and trials of Posthumus, who has endured the same kind of suffering as Shakespeare's other heroes. Jupiter is the " thunder-master " who shows his " spite on mortal flies." The helplessness of Posthumus' birth is remembered.

Mother :   Lucina lent not me her aid,
           But took me in my throes ;
     That from me was Posthumus ript,
           Came crying 'mongst his foes,
               A thing of pity !

If we consider that Iachimo is of the same kin as Iago, and that both are embodiments of the spirit of cynicism and devitalised intellectual energy which blights the faith of Hamlet and Troilus in human kind and the purposes of eternity, we can find a poignant and universal note that is generally missed in Sicilius' stanza :

Sicilius :   Why did you suffer, Iachimo,
        Slight thing of Italy,
    To taint his nobler heart and brain
        With needless jealousy ;
    And to become the geck and scorn
        O' th' other's villainy ?

I am not suggesting that Shakespeare intentionally allegorises here : but that Iago and Iachimo are products of the same potentiality in his mind or soul, and that it is exactly that potentiality that rings in the pain, the cynicism, and the loathing of the problem plays. The family of Posthumus end their chant with fervent cries that justice be done. It is man's complaint to God on behalf of those he loves. Jupiter appears and answers their complaints as follows :

Jupiter :   No more, you petty spirits of region low,
        Offend our hearing ; hush ! How dare
        you ghosts
    Accuse the thunderer, whose bolt, you know,
        Sky-planted batters all rebelling coasts ?
    Poor shadows of Elysium, hence, and rest
        Upon your never-withering banks of
        flowers :
    Be not with mortal accidents oppressed :
        No care of yours it is ; you know 'tis ours.
    Whom best I love I cross ; to make my gift,
        The more delay'd, delighted. Be content ;
    Your low-laid son our godhead will uplift :
        His comforts thrive, his trials well are
        spent.

Our Jovial star reign'd at his birth, and in
  Our temple was he married. Rise, and
  fade.
He shall be lord of lady Imogen,
  And happier much by his affliction made.
This tablet lay upon his breast, wherein
  Our pleasure his full fortune doth confine :
And so, away : no further with your din
  Express impatience, lest you stir up mine.
  Mount, eagle, to my palace crystalline.
                                (Ascends.)

As Jupiter vanishes, Sicilius makes majestic comment :
  Sicilius : He came in thunder ; his celestial breath
          Was sulphurous to smell : the holy eagle
          Stoop'd as to foot us ; his ascension is
          More sweet than our blest fields ; his royal
            bird
          Prunes the immortal wing, and cloys his
            beak,
          As when his god is pleased.

   Now, whatever we may think about the imaginative
impact of this scene as we read—we must remember that
we miss the heightened consciousness of the music that is
indicated, and the visual accompaniment of grouping and
dance—two things are certain : first, that there is nothing
whatever in the style to justify a critic who knows his
Shakespeare in enlisting the services of the incompetent
coadjutor ;   second, that, coming as it does before the
usual re-unions at the end of the play, it clearly points
the necessity of my thesis in dealing with the similar
plots of *Pericles* and *The Winter's Tale*, that these
miraculous and joyful conquests of life's tragedy are the
expression, through the medium of drama, of a state of
mind or soul in the writer directly in knowledge—or
supposed knowledge—of a mystic and transcendent fact
as to the true nature and purpose of the sufferings of

humanity. My primary intention here is not to insist on the truth of the immortality shadowed forth in these plays; but simply to indicate that they are of this mystic kind, so that we may allot them their proper place in our assessment of Shakespeare's achievement.

To-day we hear from theologians that immortality is a matter of quality and value rather than something which can be measured by time. Canon Streeter asserts that its truth can only be expressed by myth or metaphor.[8] Now the supreme value to man is always Love. What more perfect form, then, could such a myth take than that of the restoration to Pericles of his Thaisa and Marina, so long and so mistakenly supposed lost? It is, indeed, noticeable that these plays do not aim at revealing a temporal survival of death: rather at the thought that death is a delusion. What was thought dead is in reality alive. In them we watch the fine flowers of a mystic state of soul bodied into the forms of drama. The Parables of Jesus, which, through the medium of narrative, leave with the reader what is pre-eminently a sense of quality rather than a memory of events, are of the same kind. *Pericles* and *The Winter's Tale* show us the quality of immortality in terms of victorious love welling up in the beautiful plot of loss and re-union; and in *Cymbeline* an anthropomorphic theology is introduced to attempt an explanation and a valuation of the mystic fact.

IV.

The artist expresses a direct vision of the significance of life, and for his materials he uses, for purposes of imitation, the shapes, the colours, the people and events of the world in which he finds himself. But in course of the spiritual progress to which he is dedicated it may happen that the implements of outward manifestation in the physical universe become inadequate to the intuition which he is to express. Art is an extraverted expression of the creative imagination which, when introverted, becomes religion. But the mind of man cannot altogether dispense with the machinery of objectivity, and the inwardness of religion must create, or discern, its own objective reality and name it God. Conversely, the artist, in process of growth, may be forced beyond the phenomena of actuality into a world of the spirit which scarcely lends itself to a purely artistic, and therefore objective, imitation. In *Cymbeline* Shakespeare is forced by the increasing inwardness of his intuition to a somewhat crude anthropomorphism in *The Vision of Jupiter :* and this anthropomorphic theology is inimical to artistic expression. *Cymbeline* contains a personal God called in to right the balance of a drama whose plot, like that of *Pericles* and *The Winter's Tale*, is incompatible with the ordinary forms of life ; but this God, true enough to the religious intuition of the author, yet comes near to exploding the work of art in which He occurs. The form of dramatic art is necessarily extraverted and imitative ; and Shakespeare has passed beyond interest in imitation. If a last work of pure art is to be created there is only one theme that can be its fit material. A prophetic criticism could, if *The Tempest* had been lost, have nevertheless indicated what must be its essential nature, and might have hazarded its name : for in this work Shakespeare looks inward and, projecting perfectly his own spiritual experience into symbols of objectivity, traces in a compact play the past progress of his own soul. He is now the object of his own search,[9] and no other theme but that of his visionary self is now of power to call forth the riches of his imagination.

Let me recall the outline of the Shakespearean progress. In the problem plays there is mental division : on the one side an exquisite apprehension of the spiritual—

beauty, romance, poetry; on the other, the Hate-theme
—loathing of the impure, aversion from the animal kinship
of man, disgust at the decaying body of death. This
dualism is resolved in the tragedies: the Hate-theme itself is
finely sublimated in *Timon* by means of the purification
of great passion, human grandeur, and all the panoply of
high tragedy. The recurrent poetic symbol of tragedy
in Shakespeare is " storm " or " tempest." The third
group outsoars the intuition of tragedy and gives us plays
whose plots explicate the quality of immortality : the
predominating symbols are loss in tempest and revival to
the sounds of music. It is about twelve years from the
inception of this lonely progress of the soul to the
composition of *The Tempest*.

Now on the island of *The Tempest* Prospero is master
of his lonely magic. He has been there for twelve years.
Two creatures serve him : Ariel, the " airy nothing " of
poetry; and the snarling Caliban, half-beast, half-man ;
the embodiment of the Hate-theme. These two creatures
are yoked in the employ of Prospero, like Plato's two
steeds of the soul, the noble and the hideous, twin
potentialities of the human spirit. Caliban has been
mastered by Prospero and Ariel. Though he revolts
against his master still, the issue is not in doubt, and the
tunes of Ariel draw out his very soul in longing and desire,
just as the power of poetry shows forth the majesty of
Timon, whose passion makes of universal Hate a noble
and aspiring thing. These three are the most vital and
outstanding figures in the play : for Shakespeare had only
to look inward to find them. But there are other elements
that complete the pattern of this self-revelation.

Prospero's enemies are drawn to the magic island of
great poetry by means of a tempest raised by Prospero
with the help of Ariel. In Alonso, despairing, and self-
accusing, bereft of his child, we can see traces of the
terrible end of *Lear ;* in Antonio and Sebastian, the

tempter and the tempted, plotting murder for a crown, we can see more than traces of *Macbeth*. But, driven by the tempest-raising power of tragic and passionate poetry within the magic circle of Prospero and Ariel, these hostile and evil things are powerless : they can only stand spell-stopped. They are enveloped in the wondrous laws of enchantment on the island of song and music. Caliban, who has been mastered by it, knows best the language to describe the mystic tunes of Ariel :

> Be not afeard; the isle is full of noises,
> Sounds and sweet airs that give delight and hurt not.
> Sometimes a thousand twangling instruments
> Will hum about mine ears, and sometime voices,
> That, if I then had waked after long sleep,
> Will make me sleep again; and then, in dreaming,
> The clouds methought would open and show riches
> Ready to drop upon me, that, when I waked,
> I cried to dream again.   (III, ii, 144.)

The protagonists of murder and bereavement are exquisitely entrapped in the magic and music of Prospero and his servant Ariel. So, too, were the evil things of life mastered by the poetry of the great tragedies, and transmuted into the vision of the Myths. The spirit of the Final Plays also finds its perfected home in this the last of the series. Here the child-theme is repeated in Miranda, cast adrift with her father on the tempestuous seas; here the lost son of Alonso is recovered, alive and well, and the very ship that was wrecked is found to be miraculously " tight and yare and bravely rigg'd " as when it " first put out to sea." Prospero, like Cerimon over Thaisa, revives, with music, the numbed consciousness of Alonso and his companions; and, as they wake, it is as though mortality were waking into eternity. And this thought makes necessary a statement and a distinction as to the dual possible approaches to the significance of *The Tempest*.

First, we can regard it as the poet's expression of a view of human life. With the knowledge of Shakespeare's poetic symbolism in memory, we will think of the wreck as suggesting the tragic destiny of man, and the marvellous survival of the travellers and crew as another and more perfectly poetic and artistic embodiment of the thought expressed through the medium of anthropomorphic theology in *Cymbeline* that there exists a joy and a revival that makes past misery, in Pericles' phraseology, " sport." According to this reading Prospero becomes in a sense the " God " of the Tempest-universe, and we shall find compelling suggestion as to the immortality of man in such lines as Ariel's when Prospero asks him if the victims of the wreck are safe :

> Not a hair perish'd ;
> On their sustaining garments not a blemish,
> But fresher than before. (I, ii, 217.)

So, too, thinking of sea-storms and wreckages as Shakespeare's symbols of human tragedy, we shall find new significance in Ariel's lines :

> Nothing of him that doth fade
> But doth suffer a sea-change
> Into something rich and strange.
> (I, ii, 399.)

Especially, if we remember that the soul's desire of love in Shakespeare is consistently imaged as a rich something set far across tempestuous seas,[10] we shall receive especial delight in the song—

> Come unto these yellow sands,
>   And then take hands :
> Curtsied when you have, and kiss'd
>   The wild waves whist.
> (I, ii, 376.)

Commentators divide into two camps and argue long as to the syntax and sense of those last two lines : is " whist," or is it not, they say, a nominative absolute? And if not, how can waves be kiss'd? A knowledge of Shakespeare's imagery, however, is needed to see the triumphant mysticism of the dream of love's perfected fruition in eternity stilling the tumultuous waves of time. This is one instance of many where the imaginative interpretation of a poet, and a knowledge of his particular symbolism, short-circuits the travails and tribulations of the grammarian or the commentator who in search for facts neglects the primary facts of all poetry—its suggestion, its colour, its richness of mental association, its appeal, not to the intellect, but the imagination.

The second approach is this, which I have already indicated. *The Tempest* is a record, crystallised with consummate art into a short play, of all the themes I have discussed in this paper, of the spiritual progress from 1599 or 1600 to the year 1611, or whenever, exactly, *The Tempest*, was written. According to this reading Prospero is not God, but Shakespeare—or rather the controlling judgment of Shakespeare, since Ariel and Caliban are also representations of dual minor potentialities of his soul. From this approach three incidents in the play reveal unique interest. First, the dialogue between Prospero and Ariel in I, ii, where Ariel is tired and cries for the promised freedom, and is told that there is one last work to be done—which is in exact agreement with my reading of the faltering art of *Cymbeline*; second, Prospero's well-known farewell to his art, where commentators have seldom failed to admit what Professor Saintsbury calls a " designed personal allegory," and where I would notice that Prospero clearly regards his art as pre-eminently a tempest-raising magic, and next refers to the opening of graves at his command, thereby illustrating again the sequence from tragedy to myth which I have described; and third, Prospero's other dialogue with Ariel in V, i, where Ariel pities the enemies

26

of his master and draws from Prospero the words:

> Hast thou, which art but air, a touch, a feeling
> Of their afflictions, and shall not myself,
> One of their kind, that relish all as sharply,
> Passion as they, be kindlier moved than thou art?
>
> (V, i, 21.)

In poetic creation " all is forgiven, and it would be strange
not to forgive "; but the partial and fleeting flame of the
poet's intuition may light at last the total consciousness
with the brilliance of a cosmic apprehension. This speech
suggests the transit from the intermittent love of poetic
composition to the perduring love of the mystic.

Now these two methods of approach considered
separately and in sequence are not so significant as they
become when we realize that they are simultaneously
possible and, indeed, necessary. Together they are comple-
mentary to *The Tempest's* unique reality. For it will
next be seen that these two aspects when considered
together give us a peculiar knowledge of this act of the
poet's soul in the round: so that the usual flat view of it
which reads it as an impersonal fairy story—corresponding
to my reading of it as an objective vision of life—becomes
a three-dimensional understanding when we remember the
implicit personal allegory. Only by submitting our
faculties to both methods can we properly understand
the play to the full. *The Tempest* is at the same time
a record of Shakespeare's spiritual progress and a statement of the vision to which that progress has brought
him. It is apparent as a dynamic and living act of the
soul, containing within itself the record of its birth:
it is continually re-writing itself before our eyes. Shakespeare has in this play so become master of the whole
of his own mystic universe that that universe, at last
perfectly projected in one short play into the forms and
shapes of objective human existence, shows us, in the

27

wreck of *The Tempest*, a complete view of that existence, no longer as it normally appears to man, but as it takes reflected pattern in the still depths of the timeless soul of poetry. And, since it reveals its vision not as a statement of absolute truth independently of the author, but related inwardly to the succession of experiences that condition and nurture its own reality, it becomes, in a unique sense beyond other works of art, an Absolute. There is thus now no barrier between the inward and the outward, expression and imitation. God, it has been said, is the mode in which the subject-object distinction is transcended.[11] Art aspires to the perfected fusion of expression with imitation. *The Tempest* is thus at the same time the most perfect work of art and the most crystal act of mystic vision in our literature.

V.

An unduly personal criticism, it will be said. But that is not true. The critic who picks on this or that speech and then asserts, without due reference to other speeches or plays, that it has the final authority of Shakespeare's considered wisdom, is giving an unduly personal criticism : so, too, are those who take on themselves to decide arbitrarily that Shakespeare's intention is to show that one character more than another is justified, or that some scene or passage would not have been written save in deference to the public taste of his time ; or those whose immediate understanding of the poetry has been over much deflected from its true direction by the desire to search the world's literature and the records of contemporary events for " sources." All those are guilty of an unjust criticism, for they ever credit Shakespeare with their own tastes and aversions, and whenever they find some literary or historic tangent to the fiery circle of poetry, they think, by following its direction into the cold night of the actual, to expose the content of that burning star. But the critic who refuses the name of Shakespeare to any hypothetical figure of history but the creative impulse dynamic in the text of the plays; who yet views each play ever in its place among the completed works ; above all, who gives attention to imaginative rather than literal similarities, and refuses to be led astray by any considerations but the hot pulse of passion and poetic significance that beats within the living work of art, and alone endues it with immortality—he, by consistently aiming at a sincere and personal poetic criticism can alone hope to succeed in gaining the true objectivity of interpretation. For the poetic reality alone is the subject of his work. Therefore the conclusions of this essay, based on a close and detailed attention to poetic and imaginative fact throughout the plays, are set beyond the hostile comment of the expert on contemporary history, the tracer of " sources," and the critic who must ever think in terms of Shakespeare's " intentions." I have little to say of his intentions. Whenever I hazard a suggestion as to his awareness in uncreative consciousness of the sequence I have been tracing, I am content always to leave it a suggestion and no more. If we use the word Shakespeare in the interpretation of this sequence of plays it should be used as we use the word " God " : to signify that principle of unity and coherence within apparent multiplicity and disorder. But the necessity of recognising the significance of this sequence, and especially of these Final Plays, is, indeed, imperative.

The progress from spiritual pain and despairing thought through stoic acceptance to a serene and mystic joy is a universal rhythm of the spirit of man. William James, in *The Varieties of Religious Experience*, quotes, among other instances, the doubts and inner torments that preluded the prophetic zeal of Tolstoy's later years. His description of the state of the " sick soul " reads like a commentary on *Hamlet*[12], and it should be clear that the progress of other of his subjects from the state of sin to conversion and the conviction of salvation is but another expression of that rhythm which is to be found, too, in the progress from the Hate-theme in Shakespeare's problem plays to the mysticism of *Pericles* and *The Winter's Tale*. A curious inversion has come about. The self-abasement of the Middle Ages has developed into the satire of Renaissance Europe, and Goethe's Mephistopheles is depicted as pre-eminently the scoffer and spirit of denial. Sin has become cynicism. But the same inward movement of the spirit can be traced in its different manifestations. The work of Dostoievsky reflects it ; and Keats.[13] It need not be a progress stretched across a span of years : in Shakespeare I have traced an exact miniature of the succession of great plays to follow in the thought-sequence of one speech of *Richard II ;*[14] and the same sequence is separately apparent in some of Tennyson's early poems. As for my contention that the Final Plays of Shakespeare must be read as myths of immortality, that is only to bring his work into line with other great works of literature. Tragedy is never the last word : theophanies and reunions characterize the drama of the Greeks : they, too, tell us that " with God all things are possible."[15] Again, in *The Book of Job*, which turns on the same question as that which fires the greater plays of Shakespeare—the problem of suffering and a tragic destiny—we get again the same answer : after endurance to the end the hero has a mystic vision of God,[16] and then, in spite of reason and experience, we are told that his original wealth and happiness are restored to him tenfold. Neither *The Book of Job* nor the Final Plays of Shakespeare are to be read as pleasant fancies : rather as parables of a profound and glorious truth. The one attempts a statement of the moral purpose of God to man, in face of an apparent unconcern, offering striking parallels to the anthropomorphic theology of *Cymbeline* ; the Final Plays of Shakespeare, concerned on the whole less with a purely moral issue, and except in *Cymbeline* steering clear of definite theology, display plots whose texture is soaked in the quality of romantic immortality. For in Shakespeare, as at the conclusion of Goethe's *Faust*,[17] we are insistently aware of the quality of romantic love as in some way intrinsically connected with the immortality of the human spirit : so, too, Beatrice, not Vergil, guides Dante through the spheres of Heaven.

I have left unsaid the two most significant of all comparisons. For what is the sequence of the *Divina Commedia*, *L'Inferno*, *Il Purgatorio*, *Il Paradiso*, but another manifestation in the spatialised forms of medieval eschatology, of the essential qualities of the three groups of the greater plays of Shakespeare, *The Problems*, *Tragedies*, and *Myths* ? And what are both but reflections in the work of the two greatest minds of modern Europe—children respectively of the Middle Ages and the Renaissance—of that mystic truth from which is born the dogmas of *The Catholic Church*—the incarnation in actuality of the Divine Logos of Poetry : the temptation in the desert, the tragic ministry and death, and the resurrection of The Christ ? We should centre our attention always not on the poetic forms alone, which are things of time and history, but on the spirit which burns through them and is eternal in its rhythm of pain, endurance, and joy.

NOTES.

1 My order is close to that of the late Prof. H. N. Hudson, as given in the *New Hudson Shakespeare*. My remarks on false methods of poetic criticism do not imply any disrespect to the research and scholarship which has helped to determine the approximate order of the plays.

2 For the purposes of this paper it will suffice to start with *Hamlet* : a thorough investigation would find it necessary to include *Julius Caesar*—which probably preceded *Hamlet*—in the enquiry. I also omit *Coriolanus*, which probably followed *Antony and Cleopatra*.

3 See "Measure for Measure and the Gospels," *The London Quarterly Review*, April, 1929.

4 See "The Style of Othello," *The Fortnightly Review*, April, 1929.

5 The phrase is Mr. Middleton Murry's.

6 I am aware that this incident is in Plutarch.

7 The problem of the authorship of the early scenes of *Pericles* is a difficult one : but it is quite outside the scope of this essay since the greater part of the play and all that matters for the present thesis, is indubitably of Shakespeare's best.

8 *Reality*, page 311.

9 " Thou art thyself the object of thy search." Quoted from *The Voice of the Silence, The Varieties of Religious Experience*, p. 421.

10 I have indicated this point more closely elsewhere.

11 The words are again Mr. Middleton Murry's : see *Spiritual Vision, The New Adelphi*, Sept., 1927.

12 *The Varieties of Religious Experience*, p. 151.

13 I am thinking of Mr. Middleton Murry's interpretative work on *Dostoievsky and Keats*.

14 *Richard II*, v, v, 1-41.

15 There be many shapes of mystery ;
And many things God brings to be,
    Past hope or fear.
And the end men looked for cometh not,
And a path is there where no man thought.
    So hath it fallen here.
    (Prof. Gilbert Murray's translation of the *Alcestis*.)

16 " No new theoretical knowledge concerning God and His ways has been given to Job, but in direct intuition he has seen God face to face, and that is enough. This mystical solution is the only solution the author of the poem has to give to the mysterious problem of the Divine Providence." (The Rev. Robert S. Franks, in Prof. Peake's *Commentary on the Bible*, p. 365.) But the " mystical solution " must be taken to include and explain the meaning of Job's miraculous restoration to happiness.

17 Chorus Mysticus :   Alles Vergängliche
                   Ist nur ein Gleichnis ;
                   Das Unzulängliche,
                   Hier wird's Ereignis ;
                   Das Unbeschreibliche,
                   Hier ist es gethan ;
                   Das Ewig-Weibliche
                   Zieht uns hinan.
       (The final lines of *Faust*, Part II.)